Longman Nature Guides

Garden
Birds
of Britain and Europe

D0488886

Longman

Longman Group UK Limited
Longman House, Burnt Mill, Harlow,
Essex CM20 2JE, England

Originally published in German by
Gräfe und Unzer GmbH, München
© Gräfe und Unzer GmbH, München

English language edition © Longman Group Limited 1986

First published by Longman Group Limited 1986
Reprinted 1988

Garden birds of Britain and Europe.—(Longman nature guides)
1. Birds—Great Britain   2. Garden fauna—
Great Britain
598.2941   QL690.G7

ISBN 0-582-89317-8

Set in 'Monophoto' Photina by
Servis Filmsetting Limited, Manchester
Produced by Longman Group (FE) Ltd
Printed in Hong Kong

Picture acknowledgements:
Aquila/Wilkes: 17, 21, 33, 38; Bink: 23; Czimmek: 31; Danegger: inside
front cover, 18, 20, 24, 30, 37, 43, 44, 46, 56, 61, 69 top; Diedrich: 48;
Helo: 15; Irsch: 73 top left, 75, bottom right; Layer: 45; Leinonen: 29,
34, 42 top, 47, 52; Limbrunner: 25, 26, 27, 49; Möller: 57; Moosrainer:
10, 41; Naturalis/Reinhard: 59; Reinhard: 55, 58; Schrempp: 73, top
right, 75 top left, top right, bottom left; Schwammberger: 73, bottom left,
75 centre right; Singer: 14, 63, 66, 67; Synatzschke: 73 centre right,
bottom right, 75 centre right; Trotschel: 8; Weber: 4, 6, 68; Wothe: 5, 7,
9, 11, 12, 13, 19, 22, 28, 32, 35, 36, 39, 40, 42 bottom, 50, 51, 53, 54,
62, 64, top, bottom, 65, 69 bottom; Zeininger: 16; Ziesler: 60.

Foreword

In this truly pocket-sized bird guide you will find most of the birds you are likely to encounter in gardens, towns, parks and the nearby countryside, plus a few more. The 80 photographs in natural colours show songbirds like Blackbirds, Tits, Finches and the Starling, plus the kinds of birds of prey and waterfowl you might see in the larger parks and on lakes. The young of birds are not always like their parents and may be hard to identify, but to help you do so there are two pages of colour photographs of fledglings at the back of the guide.

Many of our common native birds are species that can live happily in proximity to man, finding food as a result of man's activities, or good places to nest in gardens. Anyone who wishes to encourage birds near their home and help them in cold and snowy weather, can find some tips on pages 70 and 74 on the right kinds of food for birds, and the kinds of nest-boxes and feeding tables to provide for them. On pages 71 and 77 are some ideas for bird tables and nest-boxes and details of how to construct them.

Unfortunately, feeding threatened birds is not by itself enough to save them. As well as the natural hazards of life such as severe weather there are the man-made hazards. These include the destruction of habitat by the felling of trees, the drainage of wetlands, and the building of roads, houses and factories. But it is possible to help birds survive, by creating within our gardens a rich habitat for them. Planting hedges, shrubs and trees for shelter and nesting, and putting in the kinds of plants which birds can use as food, will all help to create a substitute 'natural' environment.

If you make a garden attractive to birds you will have the chance to appreciate, at close quarters, the true value of these fascinating creatures.

How to use this book

The colour key

At the bottom of each page on which a bird is illustrated there is a coloured stripe which indicates the time of the year at which you may expect to see the bird. Although many of our common birds are residents there are also some which are present for only part of the year. Some come to our latitudes to make use of the long hours of daylight during the summer. These allow them plenty of time to find the insects they need to feed their young. Others come here during the winter from their summer homes in the north, escaping from the difficulty of finding food in a frozen landscape.

Red stripe: This indicates that the bird is a summer visitor. Some undertake very long journeys during their spring and autumn migrations, and at these times they may turn up outside their normal range.

Blue stripe: This indicates that the bird is a winter visitor. Many of these occur in flocks during this period, even if they are more solitary in the breeding season.

Green stripe: This indicates that the bird is present throughout the year in Britain. Not all these birds are sedentary – they may choose to live in slightly different habitats at different times of the year. Their numbers may also be increased in winter by migrants of the same species from the continent.

These colour codes will give you a good idea of when to expect to see these birds, but living creatures are not entirely predictable, and on rare occasions you may see a species outside its normal season.

Information contained in the species descriptions

Immediately below the photograph, on the left, is the **English name** of the species. Underneath this is the **scientific name** of the species. This is always in *italics*. Close relations always have the same first name (the genus), but each species has its own second name. Immediately below the photograph on the right is the **size** of the bird in centimetres. This is the length from the tip of the bill to the end of the tail, so a long-tailed bird may appear as big by this measure as a much more bulky one with a short tail. The **family** to which the bird belongs, both the English name and the scientific name, is given on the right.

The **Description** of the bird gives salient features which may help in its identification, such as colour and appearance, and sometimes a note on behaviour when this is a help. The **Where found** section gives details of the kind of habitat in which the bird is most likely to be found. It also notes whether the bird is found throughout the country or just within a restricted area. If the bird is only present for part of the year the usual months in which it can be seen are noted, and also where it spends the rest of the year. The **Nesting** section gives the months when the bird breeds. The typical habitat for breeding and the type of place where the nest is made are also given, and also the materials used in nest construction. The number of eggs is also listed. This is the number in one brood. Probably the majority of birds with a breeding season extending over several months breed, or attempt to breed, more than once in a season. In the section on **Voice** the type of sounds produced are indicated, but such representations with the printed word can only give part of the story. **Diet** is self-explanatory, noting the main food or types of food preferred by a particular species. The sections on diet may help you decide what kind of food to provide for a particular bird visitor to the garden, just as the nesting section may help you decide how to encourage nesting.

House Martin

13 cm

Delichon urbica
Swallow family (*Hirundinidae*)

Description: Blue-black above, white below, with a noticeable white rump in flight. The tail is forked but not very long. The flight is less smooth than a Swallow's. **Where found:** In towns, over open country and farmland. It spends much time in the air and may go high in the sky. Large numbers of birds may be seen together. Summer visitor from April to October. Winters in Africa south of the Sahara. **Nesting:** Most build their mud-cup nests under the eaves of houses, usually in colonies, but a few use cliffs as nest sites. They breed from May to October, rearing more than one brood. 4–5 white eggs are laid. **Voice:** A chirp. **Diet:** Flying insects.

Swallow

19 cm

Hirundo rustica
Swallow family (*Hirundinidae*)

Description: Appears black and white to casual glance, but actually dark blue above, pale buff below, with red on the brow and throat. Long and deeply forked tail with streamers on each side. No white on top of the rump. **Where found:** Open country, farmland, often near to habitation. Usually seen in air, sometimes perched, almost never lands on ground. Often flies low. Summer visitor from April to October. Winters in Africa south of the Sahara. **Nesting:** Builds a saucer-shaped nest with mud and straw, often on a ledge of a building, or on a rafter. Relies heavily on man for nest sites. Nests singly or in small groups, from May to September, laying 4–5 eggs with darker markings. More than one brood. **Voice:** A twitter. **Diet:** Flying insects.

White Wagtail   18 cm

Motacilla alba
Wagtail family (*Motacillidae*)

Description: A distinctive little black-and-white bird with a jaunty
manner and a constantly flicking tail. The photo shows a continental bird in summer plumage. British birds, usually called **Pied
Wagtails**, have a black back. Females are greyer, and have less bib.
In winter Pied and White Wagtails look very similar, and have no
black on the chin. **Where found:** Farmland, open country, likes to
be close to water. Runs on ground, also jumps into air to catch
food. **Nesting:** Nest of twigs and leaves in a cavity. Breeds between
April and August, laying 5–6 greyish eggs. **Voice:** Loud 'tsissick' as
takes flight. **Diet:** Moths, flies, other insects.

Dunnock
14.5 cm

Prunella modularis
Accentor family (*Prunellidae*)

Description: An unassuming little bird, brown above with darker streaks and plain grey below. It is easily overlooked as it moves about, keeping close to cover and hopping in a hunched, rather mouse-like posture on the ground, often twitching its wings. **Where found:** Gardens, open woods, scrubland, and hedgerows. **Nesting:** A neat nest of moss and twigs lined with wool, and sited low in a hedge or undergrowth, is home for 4–5 blue eggs. Breeds from April to July. Frequently chosen as host species by Cuckoo. **Voice:** A rather thin tinkling song, which may be heard nearly all the year. Also calls, a persistent 'tseep'. **Diet:** Insects, mites, spiders, various small seeds.

Icterine Warbler 13.5 cm

Hippolais icterina
Warbler family (*Sylviidae*)

Description: Greenish-grey above and yellowish below, the colours
dulling as autumn approaches. A pale patch shows on the closed
wings. A pointed bill. **Where found:** On the continent is common in
woods, parks and gardens, hunting actively through the undergrowth. In Britain it is rare, usually just occurring as a migrant on
passage, although on occasion it has attempted to breed. It is a
summer visitor to Europe from May until August, wintering in
tropical Africa. **Nesting:** Breeds in May and June, making a nest cup
of grass and moss some 2 m from the ground. 4–5 eggs, pinkish
with darker markings. **Voice:** Chuckling and grating noises, and
musical 'dederoid' song. **Diet:** Insects, spiders.

Lesser Whitethroat

13.5 cm

Sylvia curruca
Warbler family (*Sylviidae*)

Description: Grey-brown above, with a darker patch through eye and 'ear'. Breast whitish-grey. Throat white. (The Whitethroat *Sylvia communis* is a browner bird). **Where found:** Rather open areas where there are patches of thick cover, thorn-bushes, brambles and other scrub. Also hedgerows. A summer visitor from April to October, breeding in south-east England and elsewhere, but usually absent from Scotland. Winters in north Africa. **Nesting:** Breeds from May to July, laying 4–6 eggs, white with brown and yellow marks, in a cup-shaped nest often decorated with cobwebs. **Voice:** A 'tack, tack' alarm note. Song a rattle preceded by a soft warble. **Diet:** Insects and their larvae, some berries in autumn.

Blackcap

14 cm

Sylvia atricapilla
Warbler family (*Sylviidae*)

Description: Male has a glossy black cap, that of the female is reddish-brown. Otherwise drab. Olive-brown above, with a greyish breast and cheek. Rather slim. **Where found:** In gardens, parks and woodland, usually keeping close to the cover of trees and bushes. Flights are usually short. A summer visitor from April to October, it rarely reaches northern Scotland. It winters in southern Europe and north Africa. **Nesting:** Breeds from April to July. The nest is slung between twigs in evergreen shrubs or brambles, often low down. 4–6 marbled buff eggs. **Voice:** A melodious rich warble, usually from cover, A 'tack, tack' alarm call. **Diet:** Insects and their larvae, also fond of some berries.

Garden Warbler
14 cm

Sylvia borin
Warbler family (*Sylviidae*)

Description: Very dull plumage without distinguishing features, but rather plump and round-headed in silhouette, with a beak which is shorter than many warblers. **Where found:** In woodlands, parks, gardens, heathland and shrubby commons. Stays within cover most of the time, difficult to see although an active bird. Summer visitor from May to September, but does not reach north-west Scotland. Winters in tropical Africa. **Nesting:** Breeds in May and June, making a cup of grass near the ground for the 4–5 marbled whitish eggs. **Voice:** A pleasant warbling song, rather like Blackcap's. A sharp 'tack' call. **Diet:** Small insects picked from leaves, some berries.

Chiffchaff

11 cm

Phylloscopus collybita
Warbler family (*Sylviidae*)

Description: Greenish-grey above, lighter, yellowish underparts. A pale stripe runs above the eye. Blackish legs. **Where found:** In all types of mature woodland with undergrowth, woodland edges and hedgerows with well-grown trees. Usually feeds high up. Summer visitor from March to October to most of Britain. A few overwinter here. Most winter in the Mediterranean area. **Nesting:** Breeds from April to June, making a rounded nest of grass and dried leaves, with a side entrance. Usually 6 white eggs with darker markings. **Voice:** A double-note, repeated song, 'chiff-chaff', which distinguishes it from the very similar Willow Warbler. Alarm note a low 'hweet'. **Diet:** Picks insects and spiders from foliage, or flies up to catch insects.

Summer visitor   **12**

Willow Warbler   11 cm

Phylloscopus trochilus
Warbler family (*Sylviidae*)

Description: Very similar to Chiffchaff, but usually brighter plumage and lighter legs, and slightly longer wings. **Where found:** In
woodlands, hedgerows, parks, gardens, heathland and scrub where
there are bushes and plenty of ground cover. Often feeds low down
in bushes and small trees. Summer visitor from April to October;
perhaps our most numerous summer migrant. Winters in southern
Africa. **Nesting:** Breeds from April to July, laying 6 or 7 densely
marked white eggs in a domed nest of grass and moss. It is usually
on the ground. **Voice:** The song rises in pitch, then descends in a
musical liquid warble, quite unlike Chiffchaff. A 'hweet' call rather
like Chiffchaff. **Diet:** Insects picked from the surfaces of leaves.

Spotted Flycatcher 14 cm

Muscicapa striata
Flycatcher family (*Muscicapidae*)

Description: Not really spotted, in spite of its name. Brown above, with some streaking on the head, and a paler breast with dark streaks. Flat bill. Looks rather upright as it perches. Often takes flight to hunt and returns to the same perch. **Where found:** In parks, gardens and open woodland throughout Britain, as a summer visitor from April to September. It winters in Africa south of the Sahara. **Nesting:** Breeds from May to July, laying 4–5 pale blue eggs with darker markings, in a rather untidy nest of loose moss, hair and feathers. **Voice:** A squeaky song, a 'tsee' call. **Diet:** Insects, usually caught in flight.

Pied Flycatcher   13 cm

Ficedula hypoleuca
Flycatcher family (*Muscicapidae*)

Description: The male is brownish-black and white; the female is
brown and white, with a less conspicuous wing-bar. Smaller and
rounder than a Spotted Flycatcher it has similar hunting habits,
but is less often seen returning again and again to the same perch.
Where found: Mainly in deciduous woodland in the valleys of up-
land areas of north and west Britain. It is a summer visitor from
April to September, and winters in tropical Africa. **Nesting:** Breeds
from April to June, usually in a hole in a tree, sometimes in rock
crevices. Up to 8 green-blue eggs are laid, in a nest of dead leaves,
moss and fibres. **Voice:** Short trilled song. A loud 'whit' call. **Diet:**
Insects caught on the wing.

Black Redstart
14 cm

Phoenicurus ochruros
Thrush family (*Turdidae*)

Description: The male is dark grey across back, head and breast, with a whitish patch on the wing. A bright reddish-brown tail. The female is duller, browner, but shares the same red tail. **Where found:** In Europe is found in towns, villages, along rocky coasts, on mountains. Occurs in southern England, particularly on derelict buildings, industrial and bomb sites, and quarries. Here a scarce summer visitor, from March to October. A few overwinter here, most migrate to the warmer parts of Europe, and Africa. **Nesting:** Breeds from April to July. A nest of vegetation in a hole or on a ledge, with 4–5 white eggs. **Voice:** Jangling song. **Diet:** Insects, spiders, centipedes, some berries.

Redstart

14 cm

Phoenicurus phoenicurus
Thrush family (*Turdidae*)

Description: Male has grey back, white brow, black cheeks, and orange breast. The female is grey-brown, lighter below. Both sexes have a bright red-brown tail which gives them their name. (Old English 'steort' = tail). The tail is constantly bobbed and flicked.
Where found: Deciduous and mixed woodland, also parks and gardens, sometimes in hilly country with rocks and scrub. Summer visitor from April to October, wintering in northern Africa. **Nesting:** Breeds from May to July. A nest of grass and moss, made in a hole in a tree, or crevice in rocks or a bank. Up to 8 greenish-blue eggs.
Voice: Short melodious song, rather like Robin. **Diet:** Small insects and other invertebrates, some berries.

Robin
14 cm

Erithacus rubecula
Thrush family (*Turdidae*)

Description: Plump, with little obvious neck. An orange-red breast and face, otherwise mainly brown. Juveniles have no red, but are speckled. In Britain, but not elsewhere, they are commonly very tame and approachable. **Where found:** Mainly in gardens, parks and woodland, but may occur in almost any habitat with sufficient cover. Fond of undergrowth. **Nesting:** Breeds from March to June. Nest of moss and dead leaves, often in a hole in a bank, but may be in a bush, or in an old kettle or other artificial site. 4–6 eggs, white with red markings. **Voice:** A loud warbling song, often from a prominent perch. **Diet:** Ground-living insects and their larvae, worms, some fruit and berries.

Nightingale

16.5 cm

Luscinia megarhynchos
Thrush family (*Turdidae*)

Description: Dull in colour, with brown upper parts, lighter underparts and a chestnut tail. **Where found:** Woodland with plentiful undergrowth, also commons and hedgerows where there is sufficient cover. Very shy and inconspicuous. Summer visitor from April to September, returning to tropical Africa for the winter. Becoming rarer. **Nesting:** Breeds in May and June. Nest is a rather loose structure of grass, dead leaves and hair, either on the ground or close to it, well hidden in cover. 4–6 brown eggs. **Voice:** A loud, musical and varied song, from the middle of a thicket, which may be heard both night and day. **Diet:** Insects and other invertebrates caught on the ground.

Blackbird

25 cm

Turdus merula
Thrush family (*Turdidae*)

Description: Male is black all over with a yellow bill. The female is dark brown with a yellow-brown bill. She may be plain, or noticeably mottled below. Sometimes albino or partly-white specimens may be seen. Scuffles noisily when foraging on the ground. **Where found:** Originally a bird of woodland glades and edges, the blackbird has made good use of the man-made habitat of the garden, becoming one of our commonest birds. **Nesting:** Breeds from March to July, laying 3–5 greenish eggs with brown spots. The nest is a cup of grass, leaves and plant stems, usually in a bush. **Voice:** A loud alarm call 'tchuck, tchuck', and a strong fluting song, without repetitions. **Diet:** Insects and their larvae, worms, berries, fruits.

Fieldfare

25.5 cm

Turdus pilaris
Thrush family (*Turdidae*)

Description: Brown on wings and across shoulder, grey on head and rump, dark tail. Light underside with darker spots and cream suffusion on breast. Can vary considerably in size. **Where found:** In Britain it is a winter visitor from October to April. It is resident in central and northern Europe. Seen in winter in flocks, sometimes very large, in company of Redwings, on open fields. Also along hedgerows and woodland edges on berried bushes. **Nesting:** Breeds from May to July, often in colonies. Nests several metres high in a tree or on a rock outcrop. Nest of mud and grass. 5–6 greenish eggs with darker marks. Now sometimes breeds in Scotland and northern England. **Voice:** A harsh 'tchack, tchack'. **Diet:** Invertebrates of all kinds, berries, fruits.

Song Thrush

23 cm

Turdus philomelos
Thrush family (*Turdidae*)

Description: Brown above, creamy white below, with dark brown, rather pointed, spots. Yellowish underwing. **Where found:** Woodland, parks and gardens, and other habitats where there is cover for nesting. The common 'garden' thrush, resident throughout Britain. Numbers are increased in winter by continental migrants. **Nesting:** Breeds from March to July, making a nest of twigs, moss and grass with a hard mud interior amongst foliage in a bush or tree. 3–5 blue eggs with a few black spots. **Voice:** A bright, musical song with repetition of phrases. **Diet:** Some worms, insects, fruit and berries, but particularly snails, which it smashes on an 'anvil' stone.

Redwing
21 cm

Turdus iliacus
Thrush family (*Turdidae*)

Description: Small thrush. Dark brown above, with a pale eye-stripe and 'moustache'. Pale underparts heavily streaked. Red-brown at edge of wing when standing, and under wing in flight. **Where found:** Seen on farmland and other open areas, often in company with Fieldfares, during the winter. Also in woodland. Visits from October to April, then returns to breeding grounds in Iceland and Scandinavia eastward. **Nesting:** Breeds from May to July in wooded country, often making the grass-cup nest on or near the ground. 5 or 6 dark buff eggs. Has begun to nest in Scotland in recent years. **Voice:** A thin 'tseep'. **Diet:** Worms, snails, insects, berries.

Nuthatch

14 cm

Sitta europaea
Nuthatch family (*Sittidae*)

Description: Tidy-looking, with blue-grey upper parts with a black stripe through the eye. Light orange below. A strong pointed bill. Males brighter than females. May climb trees head first downwards, as well as upwards. **Where found:** Deciduous woodlands, parks and gardens with large mature trees, especially oak and beech. **Nesting:** Breeds from April to June. The nest is made in a tree hole. The bottom is lined with dead leaves and bark. The entrance is plastered up with mud until the hole is just big enough to admit the bird. Up to 12 white eggs with brown markings. **Voice:** Repeated clear note, and a ringing 'chwitt, chwitt'. **Diet:** Insects, nuts, seeds, berries.

Long-tailed Tit 14 cm

Aegithalos caudatus
Long-tailed Tit family (*Aegithalidae*)

Description: A tiny body with a long tail. The head is rounded and the bill is short. A black and white plumage, but with a strong pink suffusion. Often gives the impression of a pink bird. British and western European specimens have a black eye-stripe. In northern Europe the head is pure white (illustrated). **Where found:** Woodlands, especially at edges or clearings, hedgerows, thickets, sometimes on scrubland. Not usually in small gardens. In winter keeps close to shelter. **Nesting:** Breeds in April and May, building a domed nest with a side entrance, out of moss, cobwebs and lichens, and lining it with feathers. Up to 12 eggs are laid. **Voice:** A thin 'tsee, tsee, tsee', and a repeated short 'tirrt'. **Diet:** Small insects, spiders.

Great Tit

14 cm

Parus major
Tit family (*Paridae*)

Description: Our largest tit. Black cap and bib with white cheeks. Black, broader in male, extends down the middle of the belly, which is otherwise yellow. Greenish back, darker tail and wingtips. Acrobatic. **Where found:** All kinds of woodland, gardens and parks. Resident all over Britain and a frequent visitor to bird tables. **Nesting:** Breeds from April to June. Nests in holes, usually low in trees, sometimes in walls and other man-made structures. Often uses nest-boxes. Up to 12 eggs, white with reddish markings, laid in a mossy cup within the nest hole. **Voice:** Very varied repertoire. A 'tink, tink' call often heard, and a ringing 'teacher, teacher, teacher'. **Diet:** Insects and their larvae, spiders, some buds, berries, seeds.

Blue Tit

11.5 cm

Parus caeruleus
Tit family (*Paridae*)

Description: Blue cap and a white face with a black stripe through the eye, also black below bill and around neck. Yellow below. Blue tail and wingtips. **Where found:** Woodlands, parks and gardens. Sometimes reedbeds. Resident throughout Britain, often in close proximity to man. **Nesting:** Breeds from April to June, laying up to 15 eggs, white with reddish markings, in a nest of moss lined with feathers situated in a hole in a tree. Uses nest-boxes. **Voice:** A 'tsee-tsee-tsee' call. **Diet:** Small insects such as aphids, caterpillars and other larvae, spiders, various tit-bits from the bird-table.

Coal Tit
11 cm

Parus ater
Tit family (*Paridae*)

Description: Small, with a black crown and bib. There is a bright white patch at the back of the neck, and white cheeks. Two white bars on the wing. Otherwise dull in colour. **Where found:** Woodlands of various kinds, but especially fond of conifers. It often searches for food up tree trunks. Resident in suitable areas throughout Britain. **Nesting:** Breeds from April to June. Nests in a cavity, often low down or on the ground, in banks, trees or walls. A mossy cup lined with hair receives from 7–12 white eggs with reddish markings. **Voice:** Rather thin. A piping 'zewi-zewi-zewi' or 'sissi-sissi'. **Diet:** Insects and their larvae, spiders, conifer seeds.

Crested Tit

11.5 cm

Parus cristatus
Tit family (*Paridae*)

Description: Small, with a raised black and white crest. Black bib, neck ring and cheek line. Otherwise pale on face and below, brown on back. **Where found:** Resident over much of the continent, but in Britain just found in the eastern Highlands of Scotland. In Britain it lives in pine forests, sometimes in other conifers. **Nesting:** Breeds in April and May, nesting in a hole or crevice in a tree which may be excavated by the female. Moss and hair make the cup to hold the 5–7 eggs, which are white with reddish markings. **Voice:** A trilling or purring call. **Diet:** Insects and their larvae, often from crevices in tree trunks, spiders, conifer seeds.

Marsh Tit

11.5 cm

Parus palustris
Tit family (*Paridae*)

Description: Black glossy cap, nape and bib. White on face below eye. Otherwise plain brown above, lighter below. (Willow Tit *Parus montanus* is very similar but with matt cap and different voice).
Where found: In spite of its name it is a bird of deciduous woodland, especially oak woods with undergrowth; sometimes in hedgerows or parkland, rarely in marshes. Resident over England and Wales, but scarcely into Scotland. **Nesting:** Breeds from April to June, laying 7 or 8 white eggs with reddish markings in a hole in tree or wall, sometimes many metres above ground. **Voice:** Several calls, a loud 'pitchoo' characteristic. **Diet:** Insects, their pupae and larvae, spiders, seeds.

Treecreeper

12.5 cm

Certhia familiaris
Treecreeper family (*Certhiidae*)

Description: A small, brown-backed, restless bird, rather mouselike in its actions as it climbs spirally up a tree-trunk before flying to the bottom of another tree to repeat the exercise. It is white beneath and has a long thin down-curved bill. **Where found:** In woodland, parks or gardens that can provide large mature trees. **Nesting:** Breeds from April to June, nesting in a crevice behind bark low on a tree, in cracks in walls, and even sheds. Nest made of dry grass, bark and hair. 4–7 white eggs with dark spots. **Voice:** A high thin 'tseee' call. **Diet:** Various insects and invertebrates gathered mainly from crevices in the bark of trees.

Wren
9.5 cm

Troglodytes troglodytes
Wren family (*Troglodytidae*)

Description: A small, rather round bird with a cocked-up tail. Dark red-brown above, lighter below, with barring on the plumage seen at close quarters. **Where found:** In undergrowth and low vegetation in a wide variety of habitats from gardens and woodlands to mountains. One of the commonest British birds, resident throughout. **Nesting:** Breeds from April to July, laying 5–6 white eggs with small red-brown marks. The nest, often in a crevice in tree or bank, is a domed structure with a side entrance, and is constructed from grass, moss and dead leaves. **Voice:** The call is harsh, 'tit-tit-tit'. The song is very loud, high and hurried. **Diet:** Small insects and their larvae, spiders, picked from leaves and ground.

Yellowhammer
16.5 cm

Emberiza citrinella
Bunting family (*Emberizidae*)

Description: Male very bright, with yellow face and underparts. Brown streaked wings, and chestnut rump. The female is much less yellow, but otherwise similar. **Where found:** In hedgerows and around farmland, on commons, heaths and scrubland. Rarely in gardens. Resident throughout Britain. **Nesting:** Breeds in May and June, laying 3–5 pinkish-white eggs with mauve marks. The nest is on or near ground level, often at the bottom of a hedge, and made of grass and moss. **Voice:** Call a metallic 'twink'. Song is supposed to resemble 'a-little-bit-of-bread-and-nooo-cheese'. **Diet:** Seeds and shoots, especially of grasses; some insects, centipedes, worms.

Chaffinch
15 cm

Fringilla coelebs
Finch family (*Fringillidae*)

Description: Male has a blue-grey cap and neck. Breast and cheeks are bright pinkish-brown. Two white bars are noticeable on its wing. Female is more nondescript, olive-brown, but has the two white wing bars. **Where found:** Very common in woods, gardens, farmland and hedgerows. In winter may be seen in open country. Resident throughout Britain. **Nesting:** Breeds from April to June, nesting in bushes, hedges, and low in trees. Makes a neat nest with grass, moss and fibres, lined with hair, and covered with cobwebs and lichens. 4–5 eggs with red-brown blotches. **Voice:** A 'pink' call. A short strong song with a final flourish 'choo-ee-oo'. **Diet:** Seeds, insects.

Brambling   15 cm

Fringilla montifringilla
Finch family (*Fringillidae*)

Description: Orange-buff breast, dark head, shoulders and wings. A conspicuous white rump. **Where found:** A winter visitor from October to April, usually seen in flocks. In woods, parks and gardens, particularly with beech trees, on stubble fields and rough farmland. Flocks mix with Chaffinches. **Nesting:** Breeds from May to July, usually from Scandinavia eastwards, in woodland and scrub. Has bred in Scotland. Nests in trees, often birch, making a lichen-covered nest and laying 6 or 7 eggs. **Voice:** A 'tchuk-tchuk' call. **Diet:** Seeds, especially beech nuts, shoots.

Greenfinch

14.5 cm

Carduelis chloris
Finch family (*Fringillidae*)

Description: Male is olive green, with yellow and black on the wings and the tail. A short strong beak. The females are much duller than males, 'sparrow-like', but have the same pattern of light splashes on side of wing and tail. A rather variable species in colour, some very green, some much browner. **Where found:** Resident throughout Britain where there are trees and bushes – gardens, parks, shrubberies and cultivated land. **Nesting:** Breeds from April to July, nesting in bushes and trees, making a rather loose nest on a foundation of twigs. Often nests in conifers. 4–6 white eggs with red-brown markings. **Voice:** Calls a nasal 'tweee' and 'chk, chk, chk'. **Diet:** Seeds, shoots and buds, insects.

Resident

36

Goldfinch

12 cm

Carduelis carduelis
Finch family (*Fringillidae*)

Description: Red face with white behind. Gold bars on wings. Black on top of head, and neck. Otherwise mainly buff. **Where found:** Open country with trees and bushes. Feeds on waste ground with weeds, scrubland, gardens and roadsides. Resident throughout Britain. **Nesting:** Breeds from May to July, nesting in spreading shrubs. 5–6 bluish-white eggs with darker markings. Nest of roots, grass and lichen, lined with hair. **Voice:** Call a liquid 'didelit'. Song a liquid twittering. **Diet:** Small seeds, especially of thistles, dandelion and other weeds, insects.

Siskin 12 cm

Carduelis spinus
Finch family (*Fringillidae*)

Description: Small. Male greenish, with yellow on face, breast and wing, and darker markings. Females much greyer, with no black on head and more streaky below. **Where found:** Woodlands, preferring conifers, but also in birches, alders and mixed woods. Resident in Scotland; in southern Britain mainly in winter, but locally present in summer. **Nesting:** Breeds from April to June, in conifer woods. Nest usually near the tip of a branch, well above ground, constructed of twigs, mosses, lichens and wool. 4–5 bluish-white eggs with darker markings. **Voice:** Twittering and wheezy calls. **Diet:** Seeds of trees and low-growing plants, insects.

Serin

11.5 cm

Serinus serinus
Finch family (*Fringillidae*)

Description: Smallest European finch. Streaked plumage, yellow rump, dark tail. Yellow face and neck in male, less yellow in female. Short bill. **Where found:** Common on continent in woodland edges, open woods, parks and gardens. Not a 'normal' British bird, but is spreading north-west in Europe; does sometimes appear here and has bred in south-east England. A summer visitor from March to October, retreating to the Mediterranean during the winter. **Nesting:** Breeds from April to July. Nest a flat saucer, placed high in a conifer near the end of a branch. **Voice:** Often used. Call a 'chirlit'. Song a jingling twitter. **Diet:** Seeds of grasses and other herbs, shoots, buds. Feeds on ground.

Linnet

13.5 cm

Acanthis cannabina
Finch family (*Fringillidae*)

Description: Male has grey head, chestnut back and in summer a
red brow and breast. Less red in winter. Female duller, no red,
mainly fawn with streaks. White patch on tail and wing. Wings
and tail proportionately long, legs short. **Where found:** Heathland,
commons, roadsides, hedgerows and gardens. Resident throughout
Britain. **Nesting:** Breeds from April to August, nesting in bushes
and low vegetation. Lays 4–6 eggs, bluish with darker markings.
Nest of grass and moss, lined with hair. **Voice:** Twitters in flight.
Song, often from the top of a bush, is a varied musical twitter. **Diet:**
Seeds of grasses and weeds, some shoots, insects.

Redpoll
13 cm

Acanthis flammea
Finch family (*Fringillidae*)

Description: A brownish, streaked finch with a red cap on front of the top of the head and a black chin. British Redpolls, 'Lesser Redpolls', are smaller and darker than some races. **Where found:** In birch, larch and fir woods, also in alder and willow. Resident in Britain but absent from some parts of the south in summer, more widespread in winter. **Nesting:** Breeds from May to July, building nests, often in colonies, in the branches of trees. Nest looks untidy, with twig foundation, but inside is snug and neat, for the 4–6 blue eggs with dark markings. **Voice:** A metallic 'tchi-tchi-tchit' call. Trilling song. **Diet:** Seeds of trees, grain, insects.

Bullfinch

14.5 cm

Pyrrhula pyrrhula
Finch family (*Fringillidae*)

Description: Chunky-looking, with a large head and not much neck. Short bill. Male (above) grey above with a black cap and bright pink breast. Female (below) a duller, pinkish-fawn. White wingbar and rump noticeable in both sexes. **Where found:** Generally keeps near thick cover, in woods, parks, gardens and hedgerows. Travels in pairs. Resident all over Britain in suitable habitat. **Nesting:** Breeds from April to July, building a nest of twigs, moss and lichen in thick cover in bushes 1 to 2 m from the ground. 4–6 green-blue eggs with spots. **Voice:** Call a soft 'peeoo'. **Diet:** Buds, flowers, berries, seeds. Some insects. Unpopular with fruit growers as it nips buds.

Hawfinch

18 cm

Coccothraustes coccothraustes
Finch family (*Fringillidae*)

Description: A large powerful finch with a very strong beak. Short square tail. Grey nape. Head and breast light red-brown, shoulders and wings darker. Black eye-patch and bib. **Where found:** Woodlands with mature trees, large gardens. Not very common and difficult to see as it is secretive and spends much time in the tree-tops. Resident, but absent from northern Scotland. **Nesting:** Breeds from April to July. Lays 4–5 eggs of rather variable colour. Nest may be very high and right out on a branch, a rather untidy shallow platform of twigs and grass. **Voice:** Call a loud, explosive 'ptick'. **Diet:** Seeds, berries and fruit, including stones of haws, cherries and sloes, which are cracked by the strong bill.

House Sparrow

15 cm

Passer domesticus
Sparrow family (*Ploceidae*)

Description: Male with dark grey crown. Black around eye. Greyish breast. Chestnut with darker markings on back. Female lacks the black throat, is duller, but has a light stripe above the eye. Very gregarious. **Where found:** Resident over all of Britain, usually associated with man in towns, villages and farms. Not often encountered in 'the wilds'. **Nesting:** Breeds mainly from April to August. Lays 3–5 blotched white eggs. Nest a rather untidy domed affair constructed of grasses and lined with feathers, typically in a hole in a wall or under eaves. **Voice:** Loud, continual cheeps and chirps. **Diet:** Seeds, scraps, insects, anything edible.

Tree Sparrow

14 cm

Passer montanus
Sparrow family (*Ploceidae*)

Description: Sexes alike, smaller than House Sparrow. Chestnut crown, black cheek spot on a white cheek, and a small black bib.
Where found: Woodlands and parks during the summer, also in flocks in open fields during the winter. Resident throughout Britain but local in the west. Generally shuns urban areas, and is rural in habits. **Nesting:** Breeds from April to August. Nest made in a hole, usually in a tree, often with many feathers. 4–6 blotched white eggs. **Voice:** Short calls, higher and sharper than House Sparrow.
Diet: Seeds, shoots, buds, fruits, soft-bodied insects.

Starling

21.5 cm

Sturnus vulgaris
Starling family (*Sturnidae*)

Description: Mainly black, with glossy sheen at close quarters, and a variable amount of spotting. Rather upright stance. Yellow bill in summer, darker in winter. Gregarious, sometimes in huge flocks. **Where found:** In most kinds of habitat, including cities and other human habitation, but originally mainly a woodland bird. Resident throughout Britain. Numbers increased in winter by large-scale migration from the continent. **Nesting:** Breeds from April to June, making a nest of straw and feathers in a hole. May use a tree, cliff or building. 4–6 pale blue eggs. **Voice:** Very varied. Many whistles and warbles. A 'tchurr' call. A very good mimic of other birds and sounds. **Diet:** Insects and their larvae, worms, snails, other small animals, berries, fruits.

Jackdaw

33 cm

Corvus monedula
Crow family (*Corvidae*)

Description: Black, with greyer feathers at the back of the head and on the neck. The light iris makes the eye noticeable. **Where found:** Open country near woodland, cliffs, often seen on rooftops and chimney-pots in towns and villages. Resident throughout Britain. Gregarious. **Nesting:** Breeds in April and May, making a nest of sticks lined with wool. Nest may be in a tree hole, in a crevice on a cliff or building, or even in a chimney-pot. 4–6 blue eggs with dark markings. **Voice:** Often calls, the high-pitched ringing 'tchack' that gives its name. **Diet:** Mainly animal, including grubs and other insects, worms, eggs, chicks of other birds. Also seeds and fruit.

Jay

34 cm

Garrulus glandarius
Crow family (*Corvidae*)

Description: Pinkish-brown, with black tail and noticeable white rump. Black and white wings with striped blue feathers on the shoulder. Light-coloured eyes. The head feathers may be raised, giving a square look to the head. Often in pairs. **Where found:** Woodland, parks and large gardens. Resident through much of Britain but absent from northern Scotland. **Nesting:** Breeds from April to June. Lays 5–6 greenish eggs with darker marks. Nests in a tree or bush, the nest bowl being woven from twigs and then lined with hair. **Voice:** Noisy. A harsh voice. Call a loud 'skaark, skaark'. **Diet:** Beetles, grubs, worms, other small animals, eggs and chicks, berries, fruit, acorns. Buries acorns in autumn for later use.

Resident   48

Magpie   46 cm

Pica pica
Crow family (*Corvidae*)

Description: Half the length is accounted for by the long tail. Rather short, round wings. Black and white pied plumage, the black showing iridescent green and blue at close quarters. **Where found:** Open country with hedges and copses, woodland, suburbs. Resident throughout Britain except northern Scotland. **Nesting:** Breeds from March to June. 5–8 eggs, greenish with dark markings. Makes a nest of sticks, lined with mud. It is roofed and has a side entrance. **Voice:** Rather harsh, typical chattering call 'chak-chak-chak-chak'. **Diet:** Many small animals, including insects and their larvae, mice. Notorious as a thief of eggs and young of other birds. Also eats carrion, seeds, nuts, fruit.

Carrion Crow

47 cm

Corvus corone
Crow family (*Corvidae*)

Description: All black, slightly glossy. A strong bill, feathered to the base. In the Highlands of Scotland and on parts of the continent the Hooded Crow may be seen – the same species but with the black on the back and breast replaced with grey. **Where found:** In all kinds of habitat throughout Britain. Carrion crows are usually seen singly or in small groups. **Nesting:** Breeds from March to June. Nests singly. Nests in trees, usually in a high fork. The nest is a bulky structure of twigs and mud, given a lining of grass or wool. 4–5 eggs, greenish-blue with dark marks. **Voice:** A croaking call, 'kraa, kraa, kraa'. **Diet:** Omnivorous. Carrion, eggs, nestlings, frogs, worms, insects, snails, fruits, seeds.

Rook

46 cm

Corvus frugilegus
Crow family (*Corvidae*)

Description: Black, with bare, light-coloured area on face at base of pointed bill. Legs have baggy feathered 'trousers'. **Where found:** Typically found in farmlands where there are tall trees. Often in large flocks. Resident throughout Britain in suitable areas, but in some places numbers have dwindled with loss of trees. **Nesting:** Breeds in March and April, laying 4–6 grey-green eggs with brown markings. The untidy nest is a pile of sticks and mud, often repaired and used in successive years, in the top of a tall tree, in a colony with others of the same type. **Voice:** Call a nasal 'caw'. **Diet:** Worms, insects and their larvae, snails, carrion, fruit, seeds.

Great Spotted Woodpecker

23 cm

Dendrocopos major
Woodpecker family (*Picidae*)

Description: Mainly black above with white patches on wings. White patch across eye and over bill. Pale breast. Bright red under tail. Male, but not female, has red patch on the back of the head. **Where found:** Woodland, both deciduous and coniferous. Also in parks and large gardens if they have enough trees. Resident throughout Britain. **Nesting:** Breeds from May to July, nesting in a hole in a large tree, often excavated where the wood has decayed. The 4–7 white eggs are laid on a base of woodchips. **Voice:** Call a loud 'tchik'. Also drums fast with beak as 'song'. **Diet:** Wood-boring grubs, also other insects, nestlings, seeds, nuts.

Green Woodpecker

32 cm

Picus viridis
Woodpecker family (*Picidae*)

Description: A red crown and nape, and a black patch across the eye. The male only has a small flash of red on the black below the eye. Yellow-grey neck and breast. Body and wings green above. Yellow on rump. Looks rather yellow in flight. **Where found:** Deciduous woodland, also heaths and open country where it may be seen on the ground. Resident throughout Britain except for northern Scotland. **Nesting:** Breeds from April to June, laying 5–7 white eggs. Nests in hole excavated in a mature tree. Woodchips are used as a lining. **Voice:** A loud laughing call. **Diet:** Wood-boring grubs, ants dug from nests, seeds, nuts.

Feral Pigeon

33 cm

Columba livia
Dove family (*Columbidae*)

Description: Usually grey, with dark bars and tips on the wings. Iridescent sheen on neck, particularly in males. Can be many colours – black, brown, bluish, white or pied. Often in large flocks. **Where found:** Cities, towns, villages, farms. Very much associated with man. The ancestral wild stock was the Rock Dove, still found on some remote rocky coasts with caves. Feral pigeon resident throughout Britain. **Nesting:** Breeds mainly in summer, but also in winter. Lays 2 white eggs, in a rough nest of straw or twigs in a crevice of a building, or on a ledge. **Voice:** Calls 'oo-ru-coo'. **Diet:** Mainly vegetable, seeds, scraps, bread, man's refuse.

Collared Dove

28 cm

Streptopelia decaocto
Dove family (*Columbidae*)

Description: A pinkish-sandy colour with a black collar bordered with white on the back of the neck. **Where found:** Suburbs and parks. Usually near habitation, but where there are plenty of tall trees. Now resident through most of Britain, but a relatively recent (1955) arrival in this country, having spread across Europe from west Asia during this century. **Nesting:** Breeds from spring until end of year. Lays 2 white eggs on a platform of sticks with grass and roots high in trees, often conifers. **Voice:** A loud 'coo-coooo-cu'. **Diet:** Mainly seeds of grasses and other low plants, picked up mostly from the ground.

Kestrel

34 cm

Falco tinnunculus
Falcon family (*Falconidae*)

Description: Often seen hunting, hovering almost motionless. Long tail and long pointed wings. Male has grey head and grey tail with a black bar. Otherwise red-brown above, lighter below, both spotted. Female is without grey, duller brown with bars. A little larger than male. **Where found:** Open country, coasts, sometimes in towns. Often hovers over motorway verges. Resident throughout Britain. **Nesting:** Breeds from April to July, laying 4–5 white eggs with red markings. Nests on ledges, also old nests of crows and other birds. **Voice:** Rather quiet, but may call a high 'kee-kee-kee'. **Diet:** Mainly voles and mice, beetles and other large insects, some small birds, worms.

Sparrowhawk
37 cm female, 30 cm male

Accipiter nisus
Eagle family (*Accipitridae*)

Description: Rounded, broad wings. Male grey above, reddish below. Female grey-brown above and lighter below. Both sexes barred on the underside. Female considerably larger. Fast, manoeuvrable flight. **Where found:** Usually in woodlands with clearings and open rides. Sometimes open country, farmland with hedgerows. Resident, mainly in north and west Britain rather uncommon in east and south-east England. Has suffered from pesticides. **Nesting:** Breeds from May to July. Lays 4–6 blotched, white eggs. The nest is made of sticks and leaves, rather untidy, usually high in a tree. **Voice:** Mews, and 'kek-kek-kek' chattering call. **Diet:** Mainly small birds taken by surprise in flight. Some mice, insects.

Tawny Owl

38 cm

Strix aluco
Owl family (*Strigidae*)

Description: A rather large round head, with dark eyes and big facial discs. Broad round wings. Mainly brown, with mottles and streaks. Nocturnal. **Where found:** Woodlands, parks and gardens with trees. Resident throughout Britain. **Nesting:** Breeds from March to June, laying 2–4 white, very round eggs. Nests in a hollow tree and does not line nest. **Voice:** Familiar hoot 'tu-whit-tuwhoo'. Also much repeated call 'keee-wick'. **Diet:** Voles and mice, some small birds, worms, insects.

Barn Owl

34 cm

Tyto alba
Barn Owl family (*Tytonidae*)

Description: A heart-shaped white face. Pale brown above, white breast below. Birds on the continent (illustration) are somewhat darker and have a buff breast. Looks very pale in flight. Long legs. Nocturnal, but sometimes seen hunting before dark. **Where found:** Resident throughout Britain except north-west Scotland, but rarer than it used to be. **Nesting:** Breeds in April and May, laying 4–6 white eggs on a floor or ledge in a barn, church tower, ruin or loft. **Voice:** An alarming shriek, also snoring and hissing sounds. **Diet:** Mice, voles and rats, some shrews, birds, insects.

Moorhen

33 cm

Gallinula chloropus
Rail Family (*Rallidae*)

Description: Brownish bird with red bill and shield above. Large greenish feet. Long toes without web or lobe. White splashes on wing. Conspicuous white underside to tail, which is constantly flicked. **Where found:** On or near fresh water of all kinds, but prefers smaller areas of water. Resident in most suitable parts of Britain. **Nesting:** Breeds from March to August, laying up to 11 buff eggs. The nest is a platform of aquatic vegetation, usually in cover such as reeds, very close to water. **Voice:** A loud 'kur-ruck' alarm call. **Diet:** Aquatic insects, small fish, shoots, seeds and fruit of waterside vegetation.

Coot

38 cm

Fulica atra
Rail family (*Rallidae*)

Description: Appears black all over except for the bill and the shield on the front of the head, which are white. Very short tail. Large feet, with lobes on the toes. **Where found:** Lakes and reservoirs. Sometimes sheltered stretches of running water. Often many together, but rather quarrelsome. Resident throughout Britain. **Nesting:** Breeds from March to August. Lays 6–9 eggs, which are buff with darker markings. The nest is a floating platform constructed of reeds and other aquatic vegetation moored in shallow water. **Voice:** A rather metallic call 'keeuk'. **Diet:** Dives for small fish and insects. Also seeds, shoots and roots of water plants.

Mallard
58 cm

Anas platyrhynchos
Duck family (*Anatidae*)

Description: Male with yellow bill, glossy green neck, white collar and brown breast. Female mottled brown. Both sexes have purplish-blue iridescent wing patch. In late summer the male has an 'eclipse' plumage coloured like female. **Where found:** In all kinds of water from small ponds to lakes, reservoirs and marshes. In winter especially may be on seawater lagoons and estuaries. Resident throughout Britain. **Nesting:** Breeds from March to August, laying 8–10 greenish-blue eggs. The nest is made of grass and stems, and lined with down. It is usually made on the ground in thick cover not far from water. **Voice:** Females quack. Males have a quieter voice. **Diet:** Shoots, seeds and roots of water plants, some insects, snails, other small animals.

Resident 62

Mandarin Duck

43 cm

Aix galericulata
Duck family (*Anatidae*)

Description: Male with bright colours. Red bill, chestnut cap, light-coloured face with long cheek feathers streaked copper, with green behind. Distinctive turned-up coppery feathers on back of the wings. Female much duller, brown mottled, with greyish head and thin white eye-stripe. **Where found:** Originally from China and Japan, introduced as an ornamental bird, now living wild in Europe including Britain. Prefers ponds and streams in wooded countryside. **Nesting:** Breeds from April to June, laying 9–12 eggs in a nest of down in a hole in a tree, sometimes many metres up. **Voice:** Rather quiet, male has a single nasal note. **Diet:** Largely waterweeds.

Tufted Duck

43 cm

Athya fuligula
Duck family (*Anatidae*)

Description: A tuft of feathers at the back of the head, short in the female (lower photo), long in the male (upper photo). Male black, with yellow eyes and conspicuous white patch on the side. Female dark brown. Dives well. **Where found:** Lakes, reservoirs, marshes. Secluded places in breeding season, open water in winter. Resident throughout Britain. **Nesting:** Breeds from May to July, laying 6–14 greyish eggs. Nest made on ground from grass and reeds lined with down, usually close to water. **Voice:** Male gives soft whistling calls, female a growling note. **Diet:** Dives for insects, snails, water plants.

Pochard
46 cm

Aythya ferina
Duck family (*Anatidae*)

Description: Male with chestnut head and black breast, otherwise mainly grey. Female is light brown, paler on throat. **Where found:** Lakes and pools which have much cover around the banks. In winter on larger lakes, sometimes on saltwater lagoons. Resident in Britain, but breeds mainly in south and east. **Nesting:** Breeds from April to June, laying 6–12 greenish eggs. Nest hidden in reeds, a pile of aquatic vegetation lined with down. **Voice:** Mostly quiet, but male makes a hoarse wheeze, female a growling note. **Diet:** Dives for food, mainly waterweeds.

Greylag Goose

76–89 cm

Anser anser
Duck family (*Anatidae*)

Description: Mainly grey, but white below the tail. Large orange bill. Pink legs and feet. **Where found:** Moorland dotted with lochs, marshes, wet meadows and farmland. Resident, mainly breeding in north-west Scotland and Hebrides, and wintering in central Scotland, but introduced elsewhere in Britain. **Nesting:** Breeds from April to June, on moorland and islands. Lays 4–6 whitish eggs. The nest is on the ground near the water, constructed of heather, grass and moss. Often in colonies. **Voice:** Honking call, and hisses at intruders. **Diet:** Grasses, grains.

Canada Goose

92–102 cm

Branta canadensis
Duck family (*Anatidae*)

Description: Brown body, lighter below, with black feet. Black head and neck with a white patch from the chin to behind the eye.
Where found: Grassland close to lakes and pools, sometimes rivers, estuaries or lagoons. Originated in Canada and brought to Europe as an ornamental bird, but now there are well-established breeding populations in Britain from escaped birds. Mainly in England and Wales. **Nesting:** Breeds from March to May, laying 4–6 whitish eggs. The nest is on the ground, a depression lined with grass and down. **Voice:** A double honk in flight, 'ker-honk'. **Diet:** Grasses, clovers, shoots, water plants, seeds.

Mute Swan

152 cm

Cygnus olor
Duck family (*Anatidae*)

Description: Large, long-necked, and all white apart from the orange bill with a black base and knob. In the female (illustrated with young) the knob is smaller than in the male. Dark feet. **Where found:** Lakes, rivers, reservoirs, lochs, saltwater lagoons, estuaries. Resident throughout Britain, but in decline in some areas, partly at least due to poisoning from anglers' lead shot. **Nesting:** Breeds from April to June, making a nest close to water from a large pile of reeds and waterweeds. 5–7 grey-green eggs. **Voice:** In spite of name not mute. Can grunt, hiss and give feeble trumpeting. **Diet:** Mainly water plants. Sometimes grass or small animals.

Black-headed Gull
38 cm

Larus ridibundus
Gull family (*Laridae*)

Description: Grey on wings and back, black wingtips, red bill and feet. Otherwise white, except for dark brown head in summer (top illustration) or a small brown ear patch in winter (bottom illustration). **Where found:** Reservoirs and refuse tips, around towns, on ploughed land, sometimes on coasts. Moorland or sand-dunes in breeding season. Resident over most of Britain. **Nesting:** Breeds from April fo July, laying 3 brown eggs with dark markings in a scrape in sand, or a grass-lined depression on boggy moors. **Voice:** Usual call a harsh-sounding 'quarrk'. **Diet:** Insect larvae, worms, fish, snails, berries, and a huge variety of offal and refuse.

Helping wild birds

As most nature-lovers will realise our wild birds are under threat at the present time from a whole host of factors. Probably the greatest single factor endangering birds, and for that matter other species, is the constant loss of habitat. As time goes on more roads and houses are built, marshes and other wetlands are drained and reclaimed, and there is less space for wild animals and plants. Even in the countryside there are changes as the varied pattern of small fields and hedges that we think of as typical English scenery is replaced. Larger fields are used with fewer hedges and a type of agriculture which grows the same crop over a large area, eliminating even the added variety that used to be produced by weeds, these being treated by efficient weedkillers. So for birds there is less space and less variety of food. What can be done about it?

It is possible for the individual to do a great deal if he or she has a garden and is prepared to make it attractive to birds. As, on the whole, things that make a garden attract birds are also features that humans enjoy, no great sacrifice is required, just a bit of forethought in the planting and planning of the garden. Even a balcony or windowsill in a town can be a magnet for birds. One of the ways in which you can help is to provide plants which can be used as food by the birds. Many berrying trees and shrubs will provide food for Blackbirds, Thrushes and some smaller birds, and in the winter may attract parties of winter visitor birds as well as helping the residents to survive. If you have space you can plant trees such as oak and beech, that bear acorns and beech nuts, and these may gather in less common garden birds such as Nuthatches, Jays and Woodpeckers. Another way to provide food plants is to allow part of the garden to become a little wild. There may be a corner which does not have to be a neat lawn, where the grass can be left to grow long until late in the summer. In such an area birds will find insects and seeds, and 'wild' plants may invade, or may even be deliberately planted. In the flower border, seeding plants such as sunflowers and michaelmas daisies give us pleasure and, if they are not tidied away too quickly in the autumn, are a source of food for birds. Other 'weed' species, if not too invasive, can also be tolerated as bird food. Open compost heaps are foraging grounds for Robins and Blackbirds after worms and insects, and if the dead leaves under the shrubbery are not cleared away they help keep the ground damp and encourage worms.

As well as food, birds need water, and this is another dwindling commodity for them. A small pond with shallow edges will bring birds both to drink and to bathe. Failing this a small drinking trough will be appreciated, and a foil container sunk into the ground is a cheap way of providing one. An important point to bear in mind with a bird drinking trough, and perhaps even more so with a bird bath, is that it should be placed out of range of cover which might hide lurking predators such as cats which could attack the birds when they are off guard. A minimum of a metre, preferably more, should be allowed as a field of view and safety distance.

Birds also appreciate shelter, whether for roosting, hiding from enemies, avoiding bad weather, or for nesting, so birds may be more likely to visit a garden that has hedges, shrubberies and some trees. Many birds, from Blackbirds to Warblers may nest in a hedge. Hole-nesting birds will probably not find rotten trees with holes in the average garden, but nest-boxes fixed to the tree-trunk make a very acceptable substitute for many species. Even the walls of houses and sheds can be improved as bird habitat by planting creepers and climbers that will clothe them and hide the nests of birds. A pile of brushwood in a corner may provide cover for a Wren or a nesting-place for a Robin.

Some berrying shrubs and small trees that birds may use as food:

Cotoneaster, Pyracantha, Barberry, Japonica, Viburnum, Snowberry, Guelder Rose, Dog Rose, Hazel, Rowan, Wild Cherry and Bird Cherry, Hawthorn, Blackthorn, Privet, Elder, Cornel, Whitebeam.

Useful hedging plants for shelter and nest sites:

Hawthorn, Beech, Privet, Barberry and many others. Conifer hedges and trees provide shelter and hidden nest sites early in the spring. Cypresses, Yew and other species may be used. Ivy, Honeysuckle, Russian Vine and Virginia Creeper are useful against walls and fences.

Helping birds to nest

Nest-boxes for birds can be bought at many pet-shops, garden centres and hardware shops. Many of these will give excellent service, but anyone, even if they are not particularly good with their hands, can make a nest-box which birds will be quite happy to use. The natural cavities which birds use are not to any standard pattern and your nest-box does not need to be a marvel of joinery. All that is required is a reasonably weatherproof cavity in which to nest – a few cracks here and there are not too serious. There is no need to use 'good' wood. In fact unplaned wood is better as it gives more grip to bird feet. Wood can be treated with preservative, but it does not have to be and it may be better to treat boxes as expendable – they will last a few seasons and then be thrown away. Cedar is quite a useful wood as it lasts, but deal or even chipboard can be used. Several nest-boxes can be cut from a single plank. Some ideas and dimensions are given on the inside of the back cover.

Nest-boxes can be placed on a tree trunk or on the wall of a house or shed. There are one or two important points to remember when siting them. They should not face south so that the midday sun heats them up. They should not face the prevailing wind. They should not be situated under a water runnel on a tree or under the drip from a roof. Apart from this they can be tried at as many different levels and situations as you like – different places may attract different bird species. Site them where predators will not have easy access.

There is no point in putting up too many similar boxes in similar situations close together. Birds space themselves out when nesting, particularly from their own species. Too many nest-boxes close together may stimulate conflict rather than successful breeding. Remember, too, that there is a limit to the number of birds an area can support. If vast numbers of young are produced it may simply mean there will be more deaths of juveniles in their first year.

There is no point in putting nesting material into boxes. Most birds will just ignore or remove this and then proceed to find material of their own choice. It may be helpful to hang up some materials – straw, short lengths of wool, hair, and so on – although it is best to avoid bright colours. Apart from this the only chore with nest-boxes is cleaning them out at the end of the nesting season, removing the nests and destroying them to prevent the build-up of parasites in the boxes.

Inside the back cover two styles of nest-box are shown. That with a hole in the front is suitable for Tits, Nuthatches and Tree Sparrows if the hole is no more than 2.9 cm diameter. A larger hole may admit House Sparrows and Redstarts. As in most gardens this will mean occupation by Sparrows you may wish to keep the smaller dimension. Sometimes, in any case, Woodpeckers or Starlings may enlarge a hole and take over. The open-fronted type of nest-box may be used by Robins, Wagtails or Spotted Flycatchers. It should have a good overhanging roof to keep out weather and predators. As well as these types of nest-box it is possible to encourage more specialized species. Barn Owls sometimes use barrels, Tawny Owls will use large boxes. Some ducks will use flask-shaped baskets. Swallows can be encouraged by providing extra ledges or beams. Boards under the eaves may encourage these and House Martins. A deep enough board will prevent the house walls from being soiled. Swallows can also be helped in their nesting by providing a muddy puddle where they can gather clay, something else which is now in short supply.

Looking after fledglings

Sometimes during the breeding season you may find an apparently helpless fledgling on the ground, calling. The golden rule in cases like this is to do nothing. Nearly always the parent is close at hand,

Fledglings 1

1 House Sparrow
Passer domesticus

2 Greenfinch
Carduelis chloris

3 Blackbird
Turdus merula

4 House Martin
Delichon urbica

5 Kestrel
Falco tinnunculus

6 Tawny Owl
Strix aluco

waiting for you to go away so that it can attend to the young. Any interference may seal the fate of the chick. The parents are much better at feeding and caring for the young than you would be. Only if it is certain that the parents have met with an accident should the difficult task of hand-rearing be attempted.

Feeding birds in the winter

Feeding birds during the difficult months of the year is one of the best ways of helping them. If you have encouraged birds to nest in your garden you in any case owe it to them to provide some of their winter needs. It is generally not recommended to provide artificial foods in the breeding season. The majority of birds, whatever they eat as adults, feed their young on insects. They should not be tempted to try them on peanuts or bread, which can damage or choke the young. In the winter, though, there are several types of food that will be welcomed. They can be provided in a variety of places, including a specially constructed bird table. Some ideas for bird tables you could make are on the pages immediately inside the back cover.

In cold weather, fat provides a concentrated source of energy, and one which most birds will be able to use. Lard and suet are relished, as are titbits such as bacon and ham rinds. Scraps of meat or cooked bones with scraps attached and marrow within are also used. Various bird 'puddings' can also be made in which ingredients such as bread or cake crumbs and currants are bound together with melted fat. These can be used in the feeding bells shown inside the back cover.

Nuts are another popular treat, full of energy and protein. Peanuts are often used, but many kinds are liked. They need to be in a squirrel-proof container or hung out of reach, otherwise the rodents will quickly dispose of them. Nuts in their shells can sometimes attract Nuthatches or Great Spotted Woodpeckers. Halved coconuts can be used, and are good entertainment as Tits perform acrobatics to get at the flesh.

Bread can be used for feeding, in moderation. It should not be new, and wholemeal is probably better than white. Grains and seeds of various kinds make a natural food supplement. Proprietary bird foods are usually good, if you can afford them. Another winter standby is oatmeal or rice, boiled then with fat poured over it, congealing into a 'cake'.

It is also possible to get live foods such as mealworms or gentles from pet shops or fishing tackle shops. These are relished by many birds and form a good means of getting Robins hand-tame.

Reject fruit such as rotten apples and peelings can also be used by members of the Thrush family.

Fledglings 2

7 Black Redstart
Phoenicurus ochruros

8 Robin
Erithacus rubecula

9 Bullfinch
Pyrrhula pyrrhula

10 Chaffinch
Fringilla coelebs

11 Goldfinch
Carduelis carduelis

12 Blue Tit
Parus caeruleus

Foods suitable for various species

Species	Large seeds & nuts	Small seeds	Suet/ lard/ fats	Oatmeal 'cake'	Stale bread	Cooked scraps
Dunnock		×	×	×		×
Robin			×	×	×	×
Starling			×	×		×
Long-tailed Tit			×	×		×
Nuthatch	×	×	×		×	×
Tits	×	×	×		×	×
Treecreeper			×			×
Wren			×			×
Yellowhammer	×	×		×		
Chaffinch	×	×		×	×	
Goldfinch		×			×	
Greenfinch	×	×			×	
Siskin		×		×		
Linnet		×				
Bullfinch	×	×			×	
Hawfinch	×					
Sparrows	×	×		×	×	×
Jay	×			×		
Woodpecker	×		×			
Doves	×	×		×		
Waterfowl				×	×	

Nest-boxes and bird-tables to make yourself

With imagination and a little work you can make yourself a good range of bird-tables or nest-boxes to fit every situation. Just inside the back cover you will find some illustrations of bird-tables, with measurements provided in case you wish to copy them. But you can make others as simple as you like, or of greater complexity, with compartments for different foods, places to hang strings of nuts and so on. They can be strictly utilitarian or can be thatched or otherwise ornamented, but it is usually better to steer clear of garish colours or fluttering or clattering accessories as these are apt to alarm the more nervous and interesting types of bird. With nest-boxes the dimensions are a little more critical, but rectangular, square or round designs can all be used. Rough-planed 2 cm wood serves well, but other thicknesses can be used, although very thin wood will soon succumb to the weather and very thick wood may make the nest-box cumbersome to hang. It is always an advantage to have easy access to the inside of the box for cleaning, and the easiest way to arrange this is to hinge the lid with a strip of water-proof cloth or rubber. Otherwise an opening can be made at the side. The size of the entrance hole will depend on the species you wish to attract.

Index